GUITAR • VOCAL

STRUM & SING

BLUES

LYRICS, CHORD SYMBOLS AND
GUITAR CHORD DIAGRAMS FOR 30 SONGS

ISBN 978-1-4950-6242-1

HAL•LEONARD®
CORPORATION

7777 W. BLUEMOUND RD. P.O. BOX 13819 MILWAUKEE, WI 53213

Visit Hal Leonard Online at
www.halleonard.com

4
Ain't Nobody's Business
FREDDIE KING

6
Before You Accuse Me
(Take a Look at Yourself)
ERIC CLAPTON

8
Blues Before Sunrise
LEROY CARR

10
Come On in My Kitchen
ROBERT JOHNSON

12
Darlin' You Know I Love You
B.B. KING

16
Don't Start Me to Talkin'
SONNY BOY WILLIAMSON

18
Every Day I Have the Blues
B.B. KING

13
Further On Up the Road
ERIC CLAPTON

20
Help the Poor
B.B. KING

22
How Long Blues
(How Long, How Long Blues)
LEROY CARR

24
I Can't Be Satisfied
MUDDY WATERS

26
I'd Rather Go Blind
ETTA JAMES

28
Ice Cream Man
JOHN BRIM

30
It Hurts Me Too
ELMORE JAMES

32
Kansas City
WILBERT HARRISON

34
Key to the Highway
LITTLE WALTER

36
Let the Good Times Roll
B.B. KING

38
Life by the Drop
STEVIE RAY VAUGHAN & DOUBLE TROUBLE

40
Love in Vain Blues
ROBERT JOHNSON

42
My Babe
LITTLE WALTER

44
Nobody Knows You When
You're Down and Out
BESSIE SMITH

46
Once a Gambler
LIGHTNIN' HOPKINS

27
Please Accept My Love
B.B. KING

48
Pony Blues
CHARLIE PATTON

50
Route 66
THE ROLLING STONES

60
Sitting on Top of the World
HOWLIN' WOLF

52
Someday, After Awhile (You'll Be Sorry)
FREDDIE KING

54
The Things That I Used to Do
GUITAR SLIM

56
Three Hours Past Midnight
JOHNNY "GUITAR" WATSON

58
The Thrill Is Gone
B.B. KING

Ain't Nobody's Business

Words and Music by Clarence Williams, James Witherspoon,
Porter Grainger and Robert Prince

(Capo 1st fret)

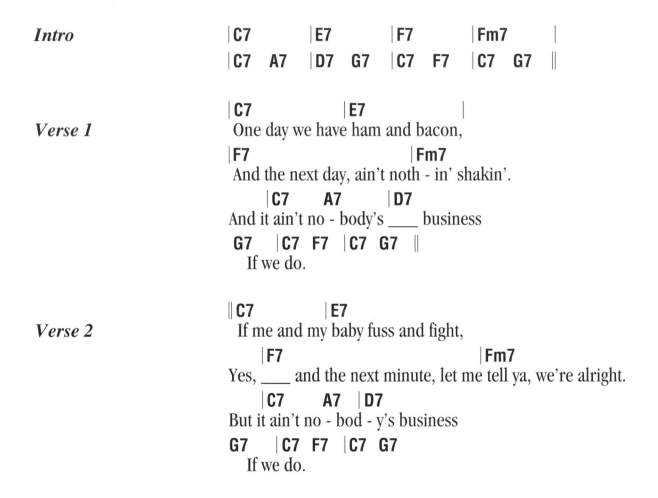

Intro

|C7 |E7 |F7 |Fm7 |
|C7 A7 |D7 G7 |C7 F7 |C7 G7 ||

Verse 1

|C7 |E7 |
One day we have ham and bacon,
|F7 |Fm7
And the next day, ain't noth - in' shakin'.
      |C7   A7 |D7
And it ain't no - body's ___ business
G7 |C7 F7 |C7 G7 ||
   If we do.

Verse 2

||C7 |E7
If me and my baby fuss and fight,
      |F7 |Fm7
Yes, ___ and the next minute, let me tell ya, we're alright.
      |C7   A7 |D7
But it ain't no - bod - y's business
G7 |C7 F7 |C7 G7
   If we do.

Verse 3

‖C7 |E7

I'm three times seven,

   |F7 |Fm7

Lord, ____ let me tell ya, that makes twenty one.

   |C7   A7 |D7

And it ain't no - bod - y's business

G7 |C7 F7 |C7 G7 ‖

  What I do.

Guitar Solo

Repeat Verse 1 (Instrumental)

Verse 4

|C7 |E7 |

 Lord, Lord, ____ Lord, Lordy, Lord,

|F7 |Fm7

 Lord, Lordy, Lordy, Lordy, Lordy

  |C7 A7 |D7

And it ain't   nobod - y's business

G7 |C7 F7 |C7 D♭9 C9 ‖

  What I do.

Before You Accuse Me
(Take a Look at Yourself)

Words and Music by
Ellas McDaniels

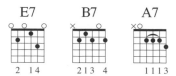

Intro

|E7 | B7 |E7

Verse 1

‖E7 |
Be - fore you accuse me,
|A7 |E7 |
   Take a look at your - self.
| |A7 |
   Be - fore you accuse me,
| |E7 |
Take a look at your - self.
| |B7 |
   You said I'm spendin' my money on other women,
|A7 |E7 | B7
   Been takin' money from someone else.

Verse 2

|E7 |
I called your mama
|A7 |E7 |
   'Bout three or four nights a - go.
| |A7 |
   I called your mama
| |E7 |
'Bout three or four nights a - go.
| B7 |
   Your mama said, "Son, don't
|A7 |E7 | B7 |
Call my daughter no more!"

Verse 3	*Repeat Verse 1*
Guitar Solo 1	*Repeat Verse 1 (Instrumental)*

Verse 4

```
|E7                          |
 Come on back home, baby.
|A7                |E7        |
    Try my love one more __ time.
|        |A7              |
    Come on back home, baby.
|                |E7        |
    Try my love one more __ time.
|              |B7                  |
    You know, I don't __ know when to quit you.
|A7              |E7    |    B7    |
 I'm gonna lose my mind!        Robert!
```

Guitar Solo 2	*Repeat Verse 1 (Instrumental)*
Verse 5	*Repeat Verse 3*

Outro

```
| E7      | A7      | E7      |        |        |
| A7      |         | E7      |        |        |
| B7      | A7      | E7      |        |       ‖
```

Blues Before Sunrise

Words and Music by
Leroy Carr

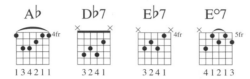

Intro |A♭ | ‖

Verse 1 |A♭ | | | |
　　　　　I have the blues before sunrise, with tears standing in my eyes.
          |D♭7 | A♭| | |
　　　　　I have the blues before sunrise, with tears standing in my eyes.
          |E♭7 | |A♭ | |
　　　　　It's such a mis'rable feeling, a feeling I do despise.

Verse 2 |A♭ | | | |
　　　　　Seems like ev'rybody, ev'rybody down on me.
          |D♭7 | |A♭ | |
　　　　　Seems like ev'rybody, ev'rybody down on me.
          |E♭7 | |A♭ | |
　　　　　I'm gonna cast my troubles down in the deep, blue sea.

Verse 3

|A♭ | | | |
Today has been such a long, lonesome day.
|D♭7 | |A♭ | |
Today has been a long, ol', lonesome day.
|E♭7 | |A♭ | |
I been sittin' here thinkin' with my mind a million miles away.

Verse 4

|A♭ | | | |
Blues starts to rollin', and it stops at my front door.
|D♭7 | |A♭ | |
Blues start to rollin', and it stops at my front door.
|E♭7 | |A♭ | |
I'm gonna change my way of living, ain't goin' to worry no more.

Verse 5

|A♭ | | | |
Now, I love my baby, but my baby won't behave.
|D♭7 | |A♭ | |
I love my baby, but my baby won't behave.
|E♭7 | |
I'm gonna buy me a heart shooting pistol,
| |A♭   E♭7 |A♭   E°7 |A♭   ‖
And put her in her grave.

Come On in My Kitchen

Words and Music by
Robert Johnson

Open A tuning, down 1/2 step:
(low to high) E♭-A♭-E♭-A♭-C-E♭

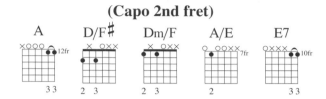

(Capo 2nd fret)

A   D/F♯   Dm/F   A/E   E7

Intro |A | D/F♯ Dm/F |A/E

Verse 1
             ||A | | |
Mmm, ___ mmm, ___ mmm, ___ mmm.
| | |
    You better come on in my kitch - en.
    | | | |
Babe, it's goin' to be rainin' outdoors.

Verse 2
|⁵⁄₄ ||⁴⁄₄A |
    Ah, the woman I love took my best friend.
    | |
Some joker got lucky, stole her back again.
    | |
You better come on in my kitch - en.
    | | | |
Baby, it's goin' to be rainin' outdoors.

Verse 3

|5/4 ||4/4 A |

Oh, ah, she's gone. I know she won't come back.

| |

I've taken the last nickel out of her nation sack.

| |

You better come on in my kitch - en.

| | ||

Babe, it's goin' to be rainin' outdoors.

Bridge

|A |3/4 |4/4 |

Spoken: Oh, can't you hear the wind howl will 'n' all?

|3/4 |

Oh, can't you hear that wind would howl?

|4/4 | |

You better come on in my kitch - en.

| | | | |

Baby, it's goin' to be rainin' outdoors.

Verse 4

|5/4 ||4/4 A |

When a woman gets in trouble, ev'rybody throws her down.

| |E7 |A |

Lookin' for her good friend, none can be found.

| | |

You better come on in my kitch - en.

| | | | |

Baby, it's goin' to be rainin' outdoors.

Verse 5

|5/4 ||4/4 A |

Winter time's com - in', hit's gon' be slow.

| | |

You can't make the winter, babe, that's dry long so.

| | |

You better come on in my kitch - en

| | | | ||

'Cause it's goin' to be rainin' outdoors.

Darlin' You Know I Love You

Words and Music by
B.B. King and Jules Bihari

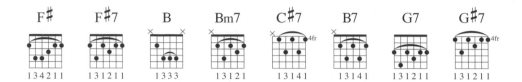

Verse 1

N.C. |F#　　　　　　|F#7　　　|B　　　　|Bm7
Now,　darlin', you know I love you and love you by my - self,
　　　　　　　　　|F#　　|C#7　　　　　|F#　B7 |F# C#7　|
But you're gone and left me for someone else.

Verse 2

|F#　　　　　　|F#7 |B　　　　　|Bm7
I think of you ev'ry mornin'　and dream of you ev'ry night.
　　　　　|F#　　|C#7　　　　|F#　B7 |F# C#7
And I would love to be with you al - ways.

Bridge

|B　　　　|　　|F#　|F#7
When night begins to fall, I cry alone,
G7 |G#7　　|　　　|C#7　|　　|
And I　wish I could hold you in my arms to - night.

Verse 3

|F#　　　　|F#7　　|B　　　|Bm7
Oh, darlin', you know I love you and love you by my - self.
　　|F#　|C#7　　　　|F#　B7 |F# C#7　|
But you're gone and left me for someone else.

Sax Solo

|B　　|Bm7　　|F#　　|F#7　　|　　|
|G#7　|　　|C#7　　|　|　|

Verse 4

|F#　　　|F#7　　|B　　|Bm7
Oh, darlin', you know I love you and love you by my - self.
　　|F#　|C#7　　|F#　B7 |F# C#7 F# ‖
But you're gone and left me, baby, for someone else.

Further On Up the Road

Words and Music by
Joe Veasey and Don Robey

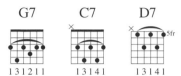

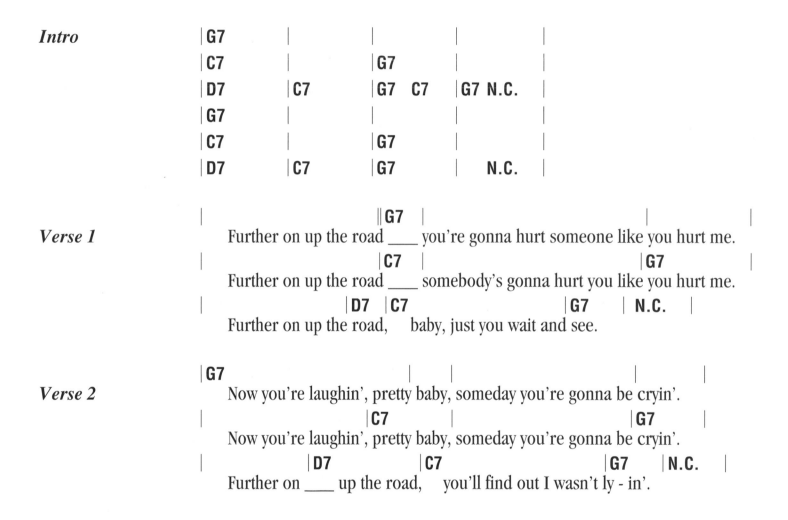

Intro

G7			
C7		G7	
D7	C7	G7 C7	G7 N.C.
G7			
C7		G7	
D7	C7	G7	N.C.

Verse 1

| ‖G7 | | |
Further on up the road ____ you're gonna hurt someone like you hurt me.
| |C7 | |G7 |
Further on up the road ____ somebody's gonna hurt you like you hurt me.
| |D7 |C7 |G7 |N.C. |
Further on up the road,   baby, just you wait and see.

Verse 2

|G7 | | | |
Now you're laughin', pretty baby, someday you're gonna be cryin'.
| |C7 | |G7 |
Now you're laughin', pretty baby, someday you're gonna be cryin'.
| |D7 |C7 |G7 |N.C. |
Further on ____ up the road,   you'll find out I wasn't ly - in'.

| |G7 | | |
Verse 3   Further on up the road ____ somebody's gonna hurt you like you hurt me.
| |C7 | |G7 |
                Further on up the road ____ somebody's gonna hurt you like you hurt me.
| |D7 |C7 |G7 | N.C. |
                Further on up the road,   baby, you just wait and see.

Guitar Solo 1   ‖: G7 | | | |
                    |C7 | |G7 | |
                    |D7 |C7 |G7 | N.C.   :‖ *Play 3 times*

| |G7 | | |
Verse 4   Further on up the road somebody's gonna hurt you like you hurt me.
| |C7 | |G7 |
                Further on ____ up the road somebody's gonna hurt you like you hurt me.
| |D7 |C7 |G7 | N.C. |
                Further on ____ up the road,   baby you just wait and see.

Verse 5   *Repeat Verse 2*

Guitar Solo 2   ‖: G7 | | | |
                    |C7 | |G7 | |
                    |D7 |C7 |G7 | :‖
                    |G7 | | | |
                    |C7 | |G7 | |
                    |D7 |C7 |G7 | N.C. |

Verse 6

|N.C. |G7 | |
 Further on up the road. Further on up the road.

| |C7 | |G7 |
Further on up the road. ___ Further on up the road.

| |D7 |C7 |G7 | N.C. |
Further on up the road. ___ Further on up the road.

Verse 7

N.C. |G7 | |
Further on up the road. Further on up the road.

| |C7 | |G7 |
Further on up the road. ___ Further on up the road.

| |D7 |C7 |G7 | N.C. |
Further on up the road   you're gonna find out I wasn't lyin'.

Guitar Solo 3

G7			
C7	|G7		
D7	C7	G7	N.C.

Verse 8

| |G7 | | |
Further on up the road ___ somebody's gonna hurt you like you hurt me.

| |C7 | G7 |
Further on up the road ___ somebody's gonna hurt you like you hurt me.

|D7 |C7 |G7 | N.C. |
 Further on,   baby, you just wait and see.

Guitar Solo 4

Repeat Guitar Solo 3 2 times

Outro

|G7 | | | |
|C7 | |G7 | | |
|D7 |C7 |G7 N.C. | G7   ‖

Don't Start Me to Talkin'

By Sonny Boy Williamson

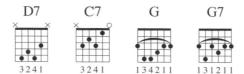

Intro

| G7 D7 | G7 D7 | G C7 | G D7

Verse 1

‖G   N.C. |G   N.C. |
Well, I'm   goin' down to Rosie's,   stop at Fannie May's,
|G   N.C. |G   N.C.
Gonna tell Fannie what I heard   her boyfriend say.
|C7 | |G |
Don't   start me talkin', I'll tell ev'rything I know.
| |D7 |
I'm gonna break up this signifyin',
|C7 |G C7 |G D7
'Cause somebody's got to go.

Verse 2

‖G   N.C. |G   N.C. |
Jack give his wife two dollars to go to downtown   and get some market.
|G   N.C. |G   N.C. |
Gets out on the streets,   ol' George stopped her.
|G   N.C. |G   N.C. |
He knocked her down   and blackened her eye.
|G   N.C. |G7
She gets back home, tell her husband a lie.
|C7 | |G |
Don't   start me talkin', I'll tell ev'rything I know.
| |D7 |
I'm gonna break up this signifyin',
|C7 |G C7 |G D7 ‖
Somebody's got to go.

Harmonica Solo

```
|G          |          |          |          |
|C7         |          |G         |          |          |
|D7         |C7        |G    C7   |G    D7   ||
```

Verse 3

|G N.C. |G N.C. |
She borrowed some money,   go to the beauty shop,

|G N.C. |G N.C. |
She honked his horn, she began to stop.

|G N.C. |G N.C.
Said, "Take me, baby,   around the block.

    |G N.C. |G7
I'm goin' to the beauty shop where I can get my hair sock."

       |C7 | |G |
Don't   start me talkin', I'll tell ev'rything I know.

| |D7 |
  I'm gonna break up this signifyin',

|C7 |G   C7 |G   D7 ||
  Somebody's got to go.

Outro

```
|G          |          |          |          |
|C7         |          |G         |          |          |
|D7         |C7        |G    C7   |G         ||
```

Everyday I Have the Blues

Words and Music by
Peter Chatman

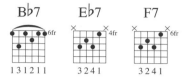

Intro

Bb7			
Eb7		Bb7	
F7	Eb7	Bb7	

Verse 1

||Bb7 | | | |
Ev'ry - day, ev'ryday I have the blues.
| |Eb7 | |Bb7 |
Oh, ___ ev'ryday, ev'ryday I have the blues.
|F7 |Eb7 |Bb7 |
When you see me worry, babe, yeah, it's you I hate to lose.

Verse 2

||Bb7 | | | |
Well, ___ nobody loves me, nobody seems to care.
| |Eb7 | |Bb7 |
Oh, ___ nobody loves me, nobody seems to care.
| |F7 |Eb7 |Bb7 |
Well, worries and trouble, darlin', babe, you know I've had ___ my share.
| ||
Oh, look out!

Guitar Solo   *Repeat Verse 1 (Instrumental)*

```
                    |Bb7        |          |          |Eb7      |
```
Verse 3   Ev'ry - day, ev'ry - day, ev'ry - day, ev'ry - day, ev' - ryday,
```
                    |              |Bb7        |
```
Ev'ryday I have the blues.
```
                    |              |F7          |Eb7           |Bb7          |
```
                When you see me worryin', babe,   babe, it's you I hate to lose.

```
                    |        ||Bb7
```
Verse 4   Oh, ____ no one loves me, nobody seems to care.
```
                    |       |Eb7        |              |Bb7        |
```
Whoa,   nobody loves me, nobody seems to care.
```
                    |              |F7          |
```
                Hey, now, wor - ries and trouble, darlin',
```
|Eb7                          |Bb7 N.C. |Bb7        ||
```
             Babe, you know I've had my share.

Help the Poor

Words and Music by
Charlie Singleton

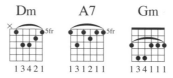

Intro

|Dm | | |

Verse 1

| ‖Dm | | |
Help the poor, ___ won't you help poor me?
| | | |A7 |
I need help ___ from you, baby, need it des - p'rately.
| |Dm |
I need you so much, I need your care
|Gm |
I need all the loving, baby, you can spare.
|Dm |A7 |Dm Gm |Dm
Help the poor, ___ oh, baby, help poor me.

Verse 2

N.C. ‖Dm | | |
Say you will, ___ say you'll help me on.
| | |A7 |
I can't make ___ it no further in this world ___ alone.
| |Dm |
Baby, I'm beggin', with tears in my eyes,
|Gm |
For your lovin', don't you realize?
|Dm |A7 N.C. |Dm | ‖
I need help, ___ oh, baby, help poor me.

Bridge

|Gm | |

You are my inspiration.

|Dm | |

You could make me be a king.

|Gm |

But, if you don't come to my res - cue,

            |A7 |

I couldn't ever be anything.

Verse 3

N.C. ||Dm | | |

Help the poor, ____ baby, help poor me.

| | | |A7 |

Have a heart, ____ won't you, baby,   listen to my plea.

| |Dm |

I lost my courage till I found you.

             |Gm |

You got what it takes, ____ baby, to pull me through.

         |Dm |A7 N.C |Dm |

Help the poor, ____ oh, baby, won't you help poor me.

Outro

| ||Dm |

I'm in trouble don't you see?

| | |

Only your love can save me.

||: | :|| *Repeat and fade*

Help the poor, help the poor.

How Long Blues
(How Long, How Long Blues)

Words and Music by
Leroy Carr

Tune down 1/2 step:
(low to high) E♭ - A♭ - D♭ - G♭ - B♭ - E♭

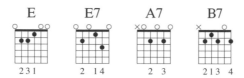

Intro

|E |E7 |A7 | |

|E |B7 |E B7 |E

Verse 1

       |E |E7 |A7 |

How long, babe, how long must I keep my watch it on?

      |E |B7 |E B7 |E

How long, how long, baby, how long?

Verse 2

         |E |E7

I'm goin' to the pawn shop, put my watch in pawn.

            |A7 |

I don't want it to tell me that you have been gone

     |E |B7 |E B7 |E

For so long, so long, baby, so long.

Verse 3

        |E |E7

I had some tuff luck lately, I got locked up in jail.

         |A7 |

I couldn't call you, baby, come and go my bail.

     |E |B7 |E B7 |E

For how long, how long, baby, how long?

Verse 4

      |E |E7
I'm goin' down to Georgia, then up to Tennes - se.
           |A7 |
So look me over, baby, it's the last you'll see of me
        |E |B7 |E   B7 |E
For so long, so long, baby, so long.

Verse 5

             |E | |E7
The last time I tried to love you, you were so very cold.
              |A7 |
I thought that I was standin', holdin' the North Pole.
      |E |B7 |E   B7 |E
For how long, how long, baby, how long?

Verse 6

        |E | |E7
I can look and see the green grass growin' on that hill,
              |A7
But I can't see the green things, only dollar bills.
        |E |B7 |E   B7 |E
For so long, so long, baby, so long.

Verse 7

       |E |E7
I haven't any money for a ticket on the train,
              |A7 |
But I will ride the rust, baby, to be with you again.
       |E |B7 |E   B7 |E E7 ‖
For how long, how long, baby, how long?

I Can't Be Satisfied

Words and Music by
McKinley Morganfield

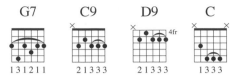

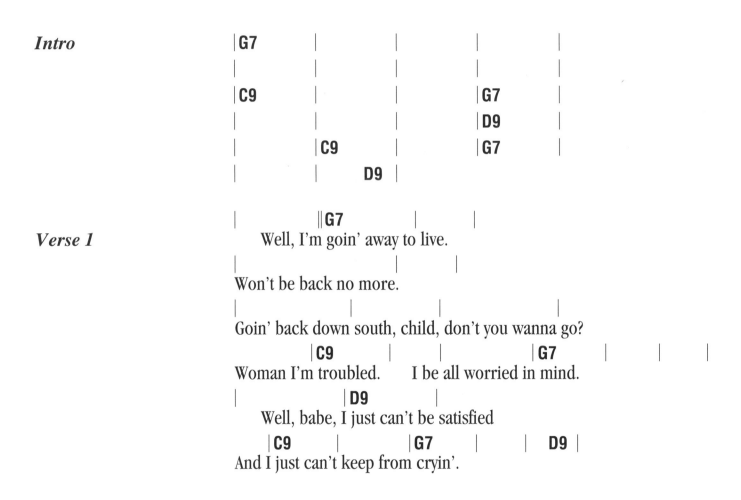

Intro

|G7 | | | |

| | | | |

|C9 | | |G7 |

| | | |D9 |

| |C9 | |G7 |

| | |D9 |

Verse 1

| ‖G7 | | |

Well, I'm goin' away to live.

| | | |

Won't be back no more.

| | | | |

Goin' back down south, child, don't you wanna go?

|C9 | | |G7 | | |

Woman I'm troubled.   I be all worried in mind.

| |D9 |

Well, babe, I just can't be satisfied

|C9 | |G7 | | |D9 |

And I just can't keep from cryin'.

Verse 2

| ‖**G7** | | |

Well, I feel like snappin' pistol in your face.

| | | |

I'm gonna let some graveyard Lord, be her resting place.

       |**C9** | |**G7** | |

Woman, I'm troubled,   I be all worried in mind.

| |**D9** |

  Well, baby, I can never be satisfied

  |**C9** | |**G7** | **D9** |

And I just can't keep from cryin'.

Slide Guitar Solo   *Repeat Verse 1(Instrumental)*

Verse 3

| ‖**G7** | |

Well, now, all in my sleep,

| | |

Hear my doorbell ring.

| | | |

Lookin' for my baby, I didn't see not a dog-gone thing.

     |**C9** | |**G7** | | |

Woman, I was troubled,   I was all worried in mind.

| |**D9** |

  Well, honey, I could never be satisfied

 |**C9** | |**G7** | **D9** |

And I just couldn't keep from cryin'.

Verse 4

| ‖**G7** | |

Well, I know my little old baby

| | |

She gonna jump and shout.

| | | |

That old train be late, man, Lord, and I come walkin' out.

  |**C9** | |**G7** | | |

I mean trouble,   I be all worried in mind.

| |**D9** |

  Well, honey, ain't no way in the world for me to be satisfied

 |**C9** | |**G7** | **C** **G7** ‖

And I just can't keep from cryin'.

25

I'd Rather Go Blind

Words and Music by
Ellington Jordan and Billy Foster

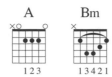

A   Bm

Intro
| A | Bm | | A ||

Verse 1
| A | Bm |
Something told me it was over
| | A |
When I saw you and her talking.
| | Bm |
Something down deep in my soul said, "Cry girl,"
| | A ||
When I saw you and that girl walking.

Chorus 1
| A | Bm |
I would rather, I would rather go blind, boy,
| | A ||
Than to see you walk away from me.

Verse 2
| A | Bm |
So you see, I love you so much,
|
And I don't wanna watch you leave me, baby.
| | A |
But most of all, I just don't wanna be free.
| Bm |
I was just, I was just, I was just sitting here thinking
| A |
Of your kiss and your warm embrace,
| | Bm |
When the reflection in the glass that I held to my lips, baby,
| | A ||
Revealed the tears that was on my face.

Outro-Chorus
||: A | Bm |
I would rather be blind, boy,
| | :||
Than to see you walk away from me.   *Repeat and fade*

Please Accept My Love

Words and Music by
B.B. King and Saul Bihari

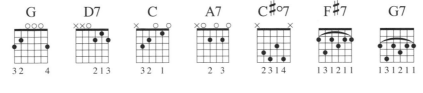

Verse 1

|N.C. |G | |D7 |
I don't even know your name, but I love you ____ just the same.
| | | |G |
Darling, let me hold your hand 'til I make you understand.

Verse 2

|N.C. |G | |D7 |
If you only, on - ly knew just how much I ____ love you.
| | | |G |
Loving you the way that I do, you'd take tonight to love ____ me, too.

Bridge 1

|N.C. |C |
I'm like the picture on the wall.
| |G |
Please don't let me fall.
|A7 |
It's my heart I'm thinkin' of,
|D7 N.C.   D7 |
So won't you please, please ac - cept my love?

Verse 3

N.C. |G | |D7 |
If you let me be your ____ slave, your love I'll cherish to my grave.
| | | |G |
And if you die be - fore I do, I'll end my life to be ____ with you.

Bridge 2

Repeat Bridge 1

Verse 4

|N.C. |G | |D7 |
If you let me be your ____ slave, your love I'll cherish to my grave.
| | | |
And if you die be - fore I do,
|N.C. | G C C#°7 |G F#7 G7 ||
I'll end my life to be with you.

Ice Cream Man

Words and Music by
John Brim

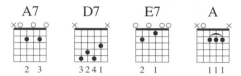

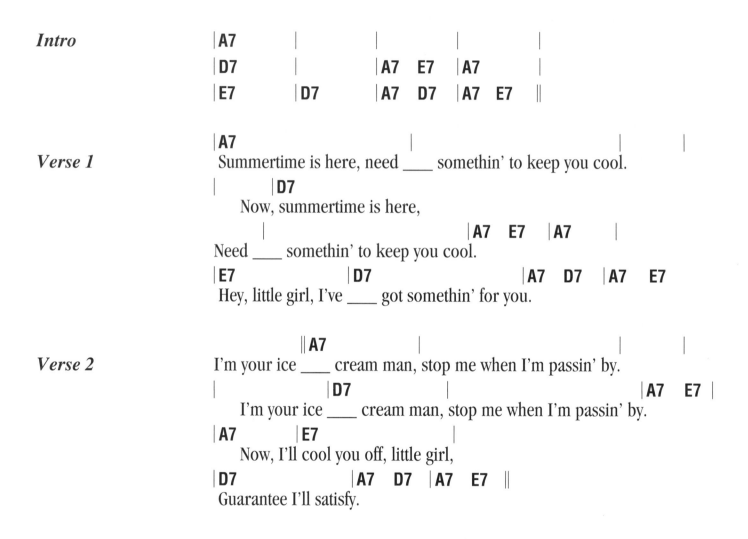

Intro

|A7 | | | |
|D7 | |A7 E7 |A7 |
|E7 |D7 |A7 D7 |A7 E7 ‖

Verse 1

|A7 | | |
Summertime is here, need ___ somethin' to keep you cool.
| |D7
Now, summertime is here,
|
Need ___ somethin' to keep you cool.
|E7 |D7 |A7 D7 |A7 E7
Hey, little girl, I've ___ got somethin' for you.

Verse 2

‖A7 | | |
I'm your ice ___ cream man, stop me when I'm passin' by.
| |D7 | |A7 E7 |
I'm your ice ___ cream man, stop me when I'm passin' by.
|A7 |E7 |
Now, I'll cool you off, little girl,
|D7 |A7 D7 |A7 E7 ‖
Guarantee I'll satisfy.

Verse 3

```
|A7  N.C.                |A7      N.C.   |
 I    got cream sandwiches, dix - ie cups,
|A7  N.C.        |A7  N.C.
 Pop - sicles and push - ups too.
          |D7             |                    |A7      |
 I'm your ice cream man, stop me when I'm passin' by.
|             |E7                  |
     Now, I'll cool you off, little girl,
|D7                   |A7  D7 |A7  E7  ‖
 Guarantee I'll satisfy.
```

Harmonica Solo   *Repeat Verse 1 (Instrumental)*

Verse 4

```
‖ A7             |              |       |
 I usually come along just about eleven o'clock.
|    |D7          |                  |A7     |
     I usually come along just about eleven o'clock.
|             |E7                      |
     Now, if you let me cool you off this time,
|D7                   |A7  D7 |A7  E7
 You'll be my reg'lar stop.
```

Verse 5

```
‖ A7             |              |       |
 I got all flavors, in - cluding pineapple, too.
|                 |D7          |                  |A7    E7 |
     Now, I got all ____ flavors, in - cluding pineapple, too.
|A7        |E7
     Now, one of my flavors, little girl,
   |D7                   |A7  D7 |A  A7  ‖
 Has got to be just right for you.
```

It Hurts Me Too

Words and Music by
Mel London

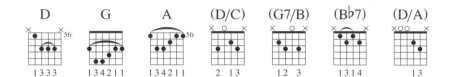

Intro

```
|D            |          |G                        |                    |
|D        |A    G  |D  (D/C) (G7/B) (Bb7) |
|(D/A)  A
```

Verse 1

```
                              ‖D                              |
```
You said you was hurting, you almost lost your mind.
```
                          |G                    |
```
Now, the man you love, he hurt you all the time.
```
                              |D                      |A
```
But when things go wrong, so wrong with you,
```
G                |D        (D/C) (G7/B) (Bb7) |(D/A)  A
```
   It hurts me ___ too.

Verse 2

```
A                        ‖D                              |
```
You'll love him more, ___ when you should love him less.
```
                          |G                    |
```
Why make up be - hind him, and take his mess?
```
                              |D                      |A
```
But when things go wrong, so wrong with you,
```
G                |D        (D/C) (G7/B) (Bb7) |(D/A)  A
```
   It hurts me ___ too.

Verse 3

      A   **|D**   **|**
He love another woman. Yes, I love you.
            |G   **|**
But you love him, and stick to him like glue.
                 |D   **|A**
But when things go wrong, so wrong with you,
G   **|D**   **(D/C) (G7/B) (B♭7) |(D/A) A**   **|**
   It hurts me ___ too.

Slide Guitar Solo

     |D   **|**   **|G**   **|**   **|**
     |D   **|A**   **G**   **|D (D/C) (G7/B) (B♭7) |**
     |(D/A) A

Verse 4

                 ‖D   **|**
Now, he better leave you, or you better put him down.
          |G   **|**
No, I won't stand to see you pushed a - round.
                 |D   **|A**   **G**
But when things go wrong, so wrong with you,
N.C.   **|**   **D**   **(D/C) (G7/B) (B♭7) |(D/A) A   D |N.C.**   **‖**
It hurts me too.

Kansas City

Words and Music by
Jerry Leiber and Mike Stoller

G7   F7   C

131211 131211 32 1

Intro | G7 | F7 | C |

Verse 1

‖ C |

I'm goin' to   Kansas City,

| | |

    Kansas City here I come.

| F7 |

I'm goin' to   Kansas City,

| | C |

    Kansas City here I come.

| G7 |

They got a crazy way of lovin' there and

| F7 | C |

 I'm gonna get me some.

Verse 2

|| C | |

I'm gonna be   standin' on the corner Twelfth Street and Vine.

| | F7 | | C |

I'm gonna be   standin' on the corner Twelfth Street and Vine,

| | G7 | F7 | C |

With my Kansas City baby and a bottle of Kansas City wine.

| | C | F7 |

Well, I might take a train, I might take a plane,

| C |

But if I have to walk, I'm goin' just the same.

| F7 |

I'm goin' to   Kansas City,

| | C |

Kansas City here I come.

| G7 | F7 | C |

They got a crazy way of lovin' there and I'm gonna get me some.

Verse 3

| C | | |

I'm goin' to   pack my clothes, leave at the crack of dawn.

| | F7 | | C |

I'm goin' to   pack my clothes, leave at the crack of dawn.

| | G7 | F7 | C |

My old lady will be sleepin', she won't know where I'm gone.

| | C | F7 |

'Cause if I stay with that woman, I know I'm gonna die.

| C |

Gotta find a brand-new baby, and that's the reason why

| F7 | | C |

I'm goin' to   Kansas City, Kansas City here I come.

| | G7 | F7 | C | ||

They got a crazy way of lovin' there and I'm gonna get me some.

Key to the Highway

Words and Music by
Big Bill Broonzy and Chas. Segar

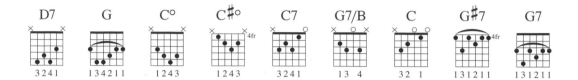

Intro
|D7 |G | C° C#° |G   D7 |

Verse 1
           |G |D7 |C7
I got the key to the high - way,   billed out and bound to go.
                    |G
I'm gonna leave ___ here runnin'.
          |D7 |G C7 |G D7
Because   walkin' is much too slow.

Verse 2
           |G |D7 |C7
I'm going back to the bor - der   where I'm better known.
                    |G
Because you have - n't done nothin',
          |D7 |G C° C#° |G D7
But drove   a good man away from home.

Verse 3

       |**G** |**D7** |**C7** |
Gimme one more kiss, mamma,   just before I go,

                 |**G** |
'Cause when I leave ____ this time, girl, I

|**D7** |**G** **C°** **C#°**|**G** **D7** |
    Won't be back no more.

Harmonica Solo   *Repeat Verse 2 (Instrumental)*

Verse 4

        |**G** |**D7** |
When the moon peak over the moun - tains
|**C7** |
    Honey, I'll be on my way.

             |**G** |
I'm gonna roam ____ this highway
|**C7** |**G** **C°** **C#°**|**G** **D7**
    Until the break of day.

Verse 5

        |**G** |**D7**
Well, it's so ____ long, so long, ba - by.
    |**C7**
I ____ must say goodbye.

          |**G**
I'm gonna roam ____ this highway
D7 |**G** **G7/B** **C** **C#°**|**G** **G#7** **G7** ‖
    Until the day I die.

Let the Good Times Roll

Words and Music by
Sam Theard and Fleecie Moore

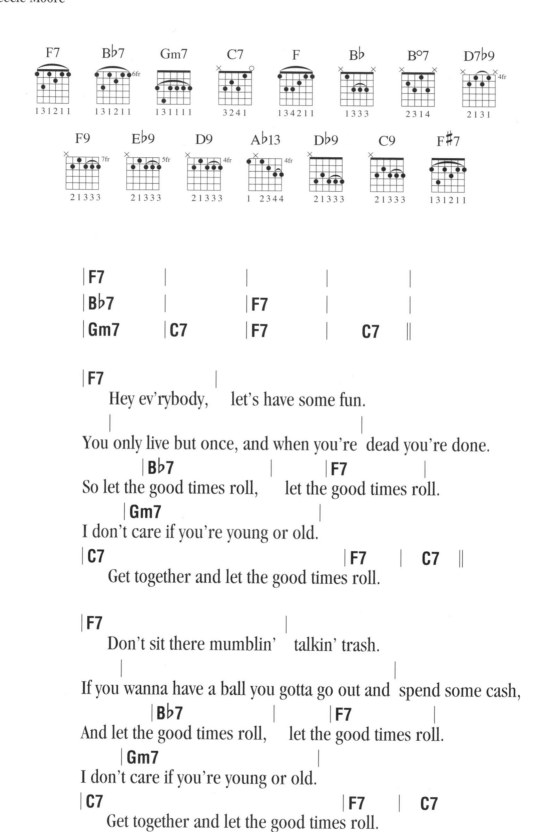

Intro

F7				
Bb7		F7		
Gm7	C7	F7		C7	

Verse 1

|F7 |
      Hey ev'rybody,   let's have some fun.
      | |
You only live but once, and when you're dead you're done.
        |Bb7 | |F7 |
So let the good times roll,   let the good times roll.
        |Gm7 |
I don't care if you're young or old.
|C7 |F7 | C7 ||
      Get together and let the good times roll.

Verse 2

|F7 |
      Don't sit there mumblin'   talkin' trash.
      | |
If you wanna have a ball you gotta go out and spend some cash,
        |Bb7 | |F7 |
And let the good times roll,   let the good times roll.
        |Gm7 |
I don't care if you're young or old.
|C7 |F7 | C7
      Get together and let the good times roll.

Verse 3

‖**F7** | |
Hey, ___ mister landlord,   lock up all the doors.

| | |**B♭7**
When the police comes around   just tell him the joint is closed.

| |**F7** | |
And let the good times roll, ___ let the good times roll.

|**Gm7** |
I don't care if you're young or old.

|**C7** |**F7** | **C7** ‖
Get together and let the good times roll.

Verse 4

|**F7 N.C.** |**F7   N.C.** |
Hey, tell ev'rybody,   Mister King's in town.

|**F7   N.C.** |**F7 N.C.** |
Got a dollar and a quarter,   just 'rarin' to clown.

|**F7   N.C** |**F7 N.C** |
But, don't let nobody   play me cheap.

|**F7 N.C.** |
I got fifty cents more that I'm gonna keep.

|**B♭7** | |**F7** |
So, let the good ___ times roll,   let the good times roll.

| |**Gm7** |
I don't ___ care if you're young or old.

|**C7** |**F7** | **C7** ‖
Get together and let the good times roll.

Verse 5

|**F** **F7** |**B♭** **B°7** |
No matter where there's   rainy weather,

|**F** **D7♭9** |
Birds of a feather gotta stick together.

|**Gm7 C7** |**F9 E♭9 D9**
So, get yourself under con - trol,

A♭13 |**Gm7 D♭9 C9** |**F7** | **F♯7 F7** ‖
Go out an' get to - gether   and let the good times roll.

Life by the Drop

Words and Music by
Barbara Logan and Doyle Bramhall

A7	A5	E5	F♯m	D5	D7(no3rd)	E

Intro   ‖ N.C.(A7) | | A5 | | |

Verse 1

‖ A5 | E5 |
Hello in there, my ___ old friend.

| F♯m | D5 |
Not so long ago it was till the end.

| A5 | E5 |
We played outside in the pour - in' rain.

| F♯m | D5 |
On our way up the road, we started over again.

Chorus 1

‖ F♯m | D5   E5 |
You're livin' out dreams of ___ you on top.

| F♯m | D5   E5 |
My mind is achin', Lord, ___ it won't stop.

| F♯m   D7(no3rd) | E   A5 | | |
That's how it happened   livin' life by the drop.

Verse 2

```
‖A5                                    |E5              |
    Up and down that road in our worn ____ out shoes.
|F#m                        |D5                |
    Talking 'bout good things and singin' the blues.
|A5                       |E5                   |
    You went your way, and I ____ stayed behind.
|F#m                        |D7(no3rd)     |
    We both knew it was just a matter of time.
```

Chorus 2   *Repeat Chorus 1*

Verse 3

```
‖A5                                    |E5              |
    No waste of time we're allowed ____ today.
|F#m                            |D7(no3rd)     |
    Churnin' up the past, there's no easier way.
|A5                            |E5               |
    Time's been between us, a means ____ to an end.
|F#m                            |D5                |
    God, it's good to be here walkin' to - gether, my friend.
```


Chorus 3

```
‖F#m                  |N.C.     |F#m                        |
    Livin' out dreams.              My mind stopped achin'.
|N.C.    |F#m          D7(no3rd)     |
              That's how it happened livin'
|E         A5     |        |        |
 Life by the drop.
|F#m            D7(no3rd)  |E        A5   |     |     |
    That's how it happened livin' life by the drop.
|F#m            D7(no3rd)  |E        A5   |       ‖
    That's how it happened livin' life by the drop.
```

Love in Vain Blues

Words and Music by
Robert Johnson

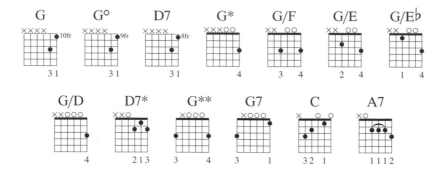

Intro |G   G° |2/4 D7 |4/4 G* G/F G/E G/E♭ |G/D   D7*

Verse 1
   ||G** |G7 | |
And I followed her to the station   with my suitcase in my hand.
| |C | |G** D7* |
   And I fol - lowed her to the station with a suitcase in my hand.
|G** |A7 |D7* |
   Well, it's hard to tell, it's hard to tell   when all your love's in vain.
|G* G/F   G/E G/E♭ G/D| D7*
   All your love's in   vain.

Verse 2
   ||G** |G7 | |
When the train rolled up to the station,   an' I looked her in the eye.
| |C | |
   When the train ____ rolled up to the station
| |G** D7* |
   And I looked her in the eye.
|G** |A7 |
   Well, I felt lonesome, I was lonesome
|D7* |
   And I could not help but cry.
|G** G/F   G/E G/E♭ G/D| D7*
   All my love's in   vain.

Verse 3

```
      ‖G**           |G7      |                        |
When the train, it left the station   with two lights on behind.
|                  |C              |
    When the train, ___ it left the station
|                        |G**  D7* |
    With two lights on behind.
|G**        |A7              |D7*                    |
    Well, the blue light was my blues    and the red light was my mind.
|G*  G/F   G/E   G/E♭  G/D |  D7*
    All my love's in      vain.
```

Verse 4

```
      ‖G**     |G7           |             |
Ou, ___ hou,    hoo, Willie Mae.
|        |C         |                 |G**  D7* |
    Oh, oh, hey,    hoo, Willie Mae.
|G**    |A7        |D7*                 |
    Ou, ou, ou, ou,    hee, vee, oh, woe.
|G*  G/F   G/E   G/E♭ |G/D   D7*  G** ‖
    All my love's in       vain.
```

My Babe

Written by
Willie Dixon

F   C   Bb   (F7)   (Bb7)   (Gm7)   (C7)

Intro

‖: F | | | :‖

Verse 1

|F | | | |
  My baby don't stand no cheatin', my babe.

| | | **C** |
Oh, yeah, she don't stand no cheatin', my babe.

| |F |
  Oh, ___ yeah, she don't stand no cheatin',

  |Bb **N.C** | |
She don't   stand none o' that mid - night creepin'.

|F | | | |
  My babe, true ___ little baby, my babe.

Verse 2

|F | | | |
  My baby, I know she love me, my babe.

| | |C | |
Whoa, yes, I know she love me, my baby.

|F |
  Whoa, yes, I know she love me.

  |Bb   **N.C** | |
She don't do nothin' but kiss an' hug me.

|F | | | |
  My babe, true ___ little baby, my babe.

Harmonica Solo

```
‖: N.C.(F7) |          |          |          |
|(B♭7)     |          |(F7)      |          |
|(Gm7)     |(C7)      |(F7)      |          :‖
```

Verse 3

```
|F                    |          |          |
 My baby don't stand no cheatin', my babe.
|                     |          |C         |
Oh, no, she don't stand no cheatin', my baby.
|F            |                  |
 Oh, no, she don't stand no cheatin',
|B♭    N.C            |          |
 Ev'ry - thing she do, she do so pleasin'.
|F            |          |          |
 My babe, true ___ little baby, my babe.
```

Verse 4

```
|F                    |          |          |
 My baby don't stand no foolin', my babe.
|                     |C         |          |
Oh, yeah, she don't stand no foolin', my baby.
|F            |                  |
 Oh, yeah, she don't stand no foolin',
|B♭    N.C            |          |
 When she's hot, there ain't no coolin'.
|F            |                  |
 My babe, true ___ little baby, she's my baby.
             |          |
True ___ little baby.
```

Outro

```
‖: F                  |          :‖
 She's my baby. (True ___ little baby.)   Repeat and fade
```

Nobody Knows You When You're Down and Out

Words and Music by
Jimmie Cox

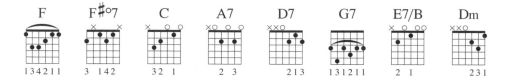

Intro |F F#°7 |C A7 |D7 G7 |C G7 C |

Verse 1
|C   E7/B |A |
Once I lived the life of a millionaire,
|Dm   A7 |Dm
　Spending my money, I didn't care.
|F   F#°7 |C   A7 |
I carried my friends out　　for a good time,
| D7 | G7 |
Buying bootleg liquor, champagne, and wine.
|C   E7/B |D7
　When I be - gin to fall ___ so low
|Dm   A7 |Dm   A7 Dm
I didn't have a friend, ___ and no place to go.
　　　　　　　　|F   F#°7 |C   A7
But, if I ever get my hands ___ on a dollar a - gain
　　　　　|D7 | G7 |
I'm gonna hold on to it till them eagle's scream.

Chorus 1

```
|C   E7/B   |A7        |Dm          A7      | Dm    |
 No  -  body  knows you    when you down and out.
|F       F#°7 |C      A7  |D7                      G7
   In my pocket, not one penny,    and my friends, I haven't any.
        |C        E7/B |A7        |
But if I ever get on my feet again,
|Dm         A7    |Dm  A7  Dm      |
  Then I'll meet my long lost friend.
|F           F#°7  |C          A7        |
   It's mighty strange,    without a doubt,
|D7                      |G7          C
   Nobody knows you when you down and out.
 |D7                |G7          C
I mean when you're down and out.
```

Trumpet Solo

```
|C   E7/B  |A7        |Dm   A7  |Dm  A7 Dm |
|F   F#°7  |C    A7   |D7       |G7     C     |
|D7  G7    |C         |
```

Chorus 2

```
|C   E7/B  A7 |Dm          A7         Dm      |
 Mmm, _____        when you down and out.
|F       F#°7 |C        A7  |D7             |           G7    |
 Mmm, ___      not one penny,    and my friends, I haven't any.
|C    E7/B        |A7            |
 Mmm, ___ I done fell so low.
|Dm        A7     |Dm        A7  Dm     |
  Nobody wants me    round their door.
|F      F#°7 |C         A7       |
 Mmm, ___      without a doubt
|D7                           G7        C
  No man can use you when you down and out.
|D7            |G7         C    ‖
I mean when you down and out.
```

Once a Gambler

Words and Music by
Sam Hopkins

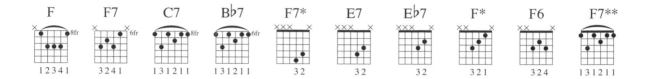

F	F7	C7	Bb7

Intro |F | |F7 | C7

Verse 1
‖F |
Yeah, you know I once ___ was a gambler,
|Bb7 |F |
But I lost my money roll.
| |Bb7 |
Yeah, you know I once ___ was a gambler,
| |F |
Lordy, but I lost my money roll.
| |C7 |
That's the reason I don't have no sweet woman.
|Bb7 |F | C7   ‖
Now I done lost my happy home.

Verse 2
|F |
You take a gambler and when he lose that no good money,
|Bb7 |F |
He sat around with his head hung down.
| |Bb7 |
When you lose that ol' dog gone money,
| |F |
You'll sit around with your head hung down.
| |C7 |
You'll try to borrow you   fifty dollars
|Bb7 |F | C7   ‖
To start all over again in another town.

Guitar Solo 1   *Repeat Verse 1 (Instrumental)*

‖**F** |

Verse 3

Baby, if you only will ___ forgive me,

|**B♭7** |**F7** |

   I won't gam - ble no more.

| |**B♭7** |

   If you only will ___ forgive me, baby,

| |**F7** |

   Ol' Lightnin' won't ___ gamble no more.

| |**C7** |

   She says I can't help you now.

|**B♭7** |**F7** | **C7** ‖

   Sold out to the devil and that's no way to go.

Guitar Solo 2   *Repeat Verse 1 (Instrumental)*

‖**F** |

Verse 4

She said I didn't want you to gamble, Lightnin'.

| | |

You know who I am,   I'm your wife.

| |**B♭7** |

She said I didn't want you to gamble, Lightnin'.

| |**F7** |

You know who I am, I am your wife.

| |**C7** |

She said lookee here brother, just like you lost your money,

|**B♭7** |**F7 F7*E7 E♭7** |**F* F6 F7**‖

You had a good chance to lose your life.

Pony Blues

Words and Music by
Charlie Patton

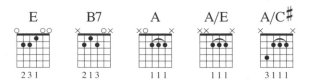

Chorus

```
|E          |          |                    | B7  |E     |
     Hitch up my pony,    saddle up my black mare.
|          |A         |                  |E  B7 |E      |
     Hitch up my pony,    saddle up my black mare.
|          |B7        |
     I'm gonna find ____ a rider,
|A/E  A/C♯  B7          |E  B7 |E  A  E |
Baby, in the     world somewhere.
```

Verse 1

```
|          ||E        |                |          |
     Ill'nois ____ and Central,   'sa matter with your line?
|A         |          B7       |E  B7 |E  A  E |
Ill'nois, Central, matter, now,  with your line?
|          |B7        |
     Come a storm ____ last night,
|A/E  A/C♯  B7         |E  B7 |E  A  E |
Torn ____ the   wires down.
```

Verse 2

```
|          ||E        |                |          |
     Got a brand - new Shetland,   man, already trained.
|A         |          |          |E  B7 |E  A  E |
Brand-new Shetland, baby, already trained.
|          |B7        |
     Just get in the saddle,
|A/E  A/C♯  B7         |E  B7 |E  A  E |
Tighten up        on your reins.
```

Verse 3

```
|                ‖E                    |
     And a brown ___ skinned woman like
|            |        |        |        |
     Somethin' fit to eat.
|A                        |
     Brown skinned woman like
|                    |E  B7 |E  A  E |
     Somethin' fit to eat.
|2/4       |4/4 B7            |
     But a jet ___ black woman,
|A/E  A/C♯    B7           |E  B7 |E  A  E |
Don't put your ___ hand on me.
```

Verse 4

```
|            ‖E        |              |        |
     Took my ___ baby,   to meet the mornin' train.
|A            |                |E  B7 |E  A  E |
Took my baby, meet the mornin' train.
|                |B7            |
     And the blues ___ come down,
|A/E  A/C♯  B7           |E  B7 |E  A  E |
Baby, like        showers of rain.
```

Verse 5

```
|                ‖E        |              |        |        |
     I got some - thin' to tell you    when I gets a chance.
|A                    |                    |E  B7 |E  A  E |
Somethin' to tell you    when I get a chance.
|      |B7            |
     I ___ don't wanna marry,
|A/E    A/C♯  B7           |E  B7 |E  A  E ‖
Just wanna      be your man.
```

Route 66

By Bobby Troup

A   D7   E7   A7

1 3 4 2 1 1   3 2 4 1   3 2 4 1   1 3 1 2 1 1

Intro
|A | | | |

Verse 1
|A |D7 |A |
Well, if you ever plan ___ to motor West,

| |D7 | |A |
Drive safe my way, that's the highway, that's the best.

| |E7 |D7 |A |
Get your kicks ___ on Route Sixty Six.

Verse 2
| |A   D7 |A |
Well, it winds from Chi - cago to L.A.

| |D7 | |A |
More than two thousand miles all the way.

| |E7 |D7 |A |
A, get your kicks on Route Sixty Six.

Bridge 1
| |A   N.C. |A   N.C. |
Well, it goes from St. Louie, down to Missouri,

|A   N.C. |
Oklahoma City looks, oh, so pretty.

|D7 | A | |
You'll see Amarillo, and Gallup, New Mexico.

|E7 | | |
Flagstaff, Arizona. Don't forget Winona,

| | |
Kingman, Barstow, San Bernardino.

Verse 3

```
                    |A          |D7                |A            |
                    Won't you get hip ___ to this kindly tip?
                    |        |D7        |          |A          |
                    If you take that California trip,
                    |                    |E7    |D7          |A          |
                    Get your kicks ____ on Route Sixty Six.
```

Guitar Solo

```
          |A          |          |          |          |
          |D7         |          |A          |          |
          |E7         |D7        |A          |          |
```

Bridge 2   *Repeat Bridge 1*

Verse 4

```
                    |A          |D7                |A            |
                    Would you get hip ___ to this kindly tip,
                    |        |D7        |          |A          |
                    And go take that California trip?
                    |                    |E7    |D7          |A          |
                    And get your kicks ____ on Route Sixty Six.
                    |                    |E7    |D7          |A          |
                    Well, get your kicks ____ on Route Sixty Six.
                    |                    |E7    |D7          |A          ‖
                    Well, get your kicks ____ on Route Sixty Six.
```

Someday, After Awhile
(You'll Be Sorry)

Words and Music by
Freddie King and Sonny Thompson

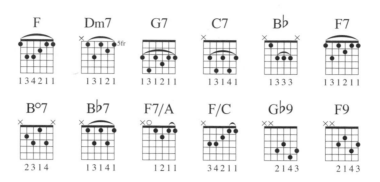

Intro

|F Dm7 |G7 C7 |F B♭ |

Verse 1

|F C7   ‖F |F7

I've got to ride that lone - some train.

|B♭ |B°7

My heart ___ is heavy with aches and pains.

|F   Dm7

But someday, ___ someday, ba - by,

|G C7 |F B♭ |

After a while   you'll be sorry.

Verse 2

|F C7   ‖F |F7

Ev'ry day my clouds are grey.

|B♭ |B°7

It takes you to roll ___ all my clouds away.

|F   Dm7

But some - day, someday,

|G C7 |F B♭ |

After a while ___   you'll be sorry.

Bridge

|F   F7   ‖B♭7

Troubles, trou - ble on my mind.

          |F

Troubles, ___ trouble way ___ down the line.

       |G7

But I don't need no ___ sympathy,

 |C7

So baby, baby, don't you pity me.

Verse 3

            ‖F |F7

I may be blue, ___ but I don't mind

     |B♭ |B°7

'Cause I know way ___ down the line.

       |F   Dm7

But, I said, someday, someday, someday, someday, baby,

|G7   C7 |F   F7/A B♭ B°7 |F/C G♭9 F9 ‖

After a while   you'll be sorry.

The Things That I Used to Do

Words and Music by
Eddie "Guitar Slim" Jones

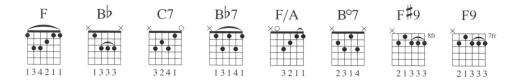

F   B♭   C7   B♭7   F/A   B°7   F♯9   F9

Intro |N.C.(C7) |

Verse 1
||F |B♭ |F |
The things that I used to do,   Lord, I won't do no more.
| |B♭ | |F | |
The things that I used to do, Lord, I won't do no more.
|C7 |
I used to set and hold your hand, baby,
|B♭ |F | C7 ||
Cry, beggin' you not to go.

Verse 2
|F |
I would search all night for you, baby,
|B♭ |F | |
Lord, and my search would always end in vain.
|B♭ |
I would search all night for you, baby,
| |F | |
Lord, and my search would always end in vain.
|C7 |
But I knew all along, darlin',
|B♭7 |F | C7 ||
That you was hid out with your other man.

Guitar Solo

```
|F        |B♭       |F        |        |        |
|B♭       |         |F        |        |        |
|C7       |B♭       |F        |        |        |
```

Verse 3

```
|F                                         ‖
```
      I'm going to send you back to your mother, baby,
```
          |B♭                    |F       |
```
Lord, and I'm going back to my family too.
```
|                                 |B♭
```
      I'm going to send you back to your mother, baby,
```
          |                       |F       |
```
Lord, and I'm going back to my family too.
```
|         |C7                               |
```
      'Cause nothin' I do that please you, baby,
```
|B♭7                       |F  F/A  B♭  B°7 |F  F♯9  F9  ‖
```
      Lord, I just can't get along with you.

Three Hours Past Midnight

Words and Music by
Johnny Watson and Saul Bihari

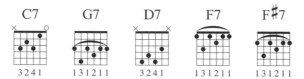

Intro
| N.C. | C7 | G7 C7 | G7 D7 ||

Verse 1

| |G7 | |
Well, here it is ___ three hours past midnight,

|C7 |G7 |
And my baby is no - where around.

| |C7 | |
Well, here it is ___ three hours past midnight,

| | |G7 |
And my baby's nowhere a - round.

| |D7 | |
Well, I listened so hard to hear her footsteps,

|C7 |G7   C7 |G7 D7
And I ain't even heard a sound.

Verse 2

        |**G7** |

Yes, ___ I tossed and tumbled on my pillow,

|**C7** |**G7** |

But I just can't close my eyes.

| |**C7** |

Yes, ___ tossed and tumbled on my pillow,

| |**G7** |

And I just can't close my eyes.

| |**D7** |

If my baby don't come back, a, pretty quick,

|**C7** |**G7**   **C7** |**G7** **D7** ||

Yes, I just can't be satisfied.

Guitar Solo

|**G7** | | | |

|**C7** | |**G7** | |

|**D7** |**C7** |**G7**   **C7** |**G7**   **D7** ||

Verse 3

| |**G7** | | |

Well, ___ I want my baby. I want her by my side.

| |**C7** | |**G7** |

Well, I want my baby, yes, I want her by my side.

| |**D7** |

Well, if she don't come home, a, pretty soon

|**C7** |**G7** **C7** |**G7** **F7** **F#7** **G7** ||

Yes, just can't be satis - fied.

The Thrill Is Gone

Words and Music by
Roy Hawkins and Rick Darnell

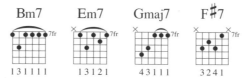

Bm7   Em7   Gmaj7   F#7

Intro

Bm7			
Em7		Bm7	
Gmaj7 |F#7 |Bm7		

Verse 1

|Bm7 | | | |
    The thrill is gone, the thrill is gone away.
|Em7 | |Bm7 | |
    The thrill is gone, baby, the thrill is gone away.
|Gmaj7 |F#7
    You know you've done me wrong, ba - by,
                |Bm7 |
And you'll be sor - ry someday.

Verse 2

|Bm7 | | | |
    The thrill is gone, it's gone away from me.
|Em7 | |Bm7 | |
    The thrill is gone, baby, the thrill has gone away from me.
|Gmaj7 |F#7 |Bm7 | ||
    Although I'll still live on, ___ but so lone - ly I'll ___ be.

Guitar Solo 1   *Repeat Verse 1 (Instrumental)*

Verse 3

|**Bm7** | | | |
The thrill is gone, it's gone away for good.
| |**Em7** | |**Bm7** | |
Oh, the thrill is gone, ___ baby, it's gone away for good.
|**Gmaj7** |**F♯7**
Someday I know I'll be holdin' on, ___ baby,
         |**Bm7** | | |
Just like I know a good man should.

Verse 4

|**Bm7** | | |
You know I'm free, free now, ba - by, I'm free from your spell.
|**Em7** | |**Bm7** | |
Whoa, I'm free, free, free ___ now, I'm free ___ from your spell.
| |**Gmaj7** |**F♯7** |**Bm7** | ||
And now ___ that it's all over,   all I can do ___ is wish you well.

Guitar Solo 2   *Repeat Guitar Solo 1*

Outro ||: **Bm7** | | | :|| *Repeat and fade*

Sitting on Top of the World

Words and Music by
Chester Burnett

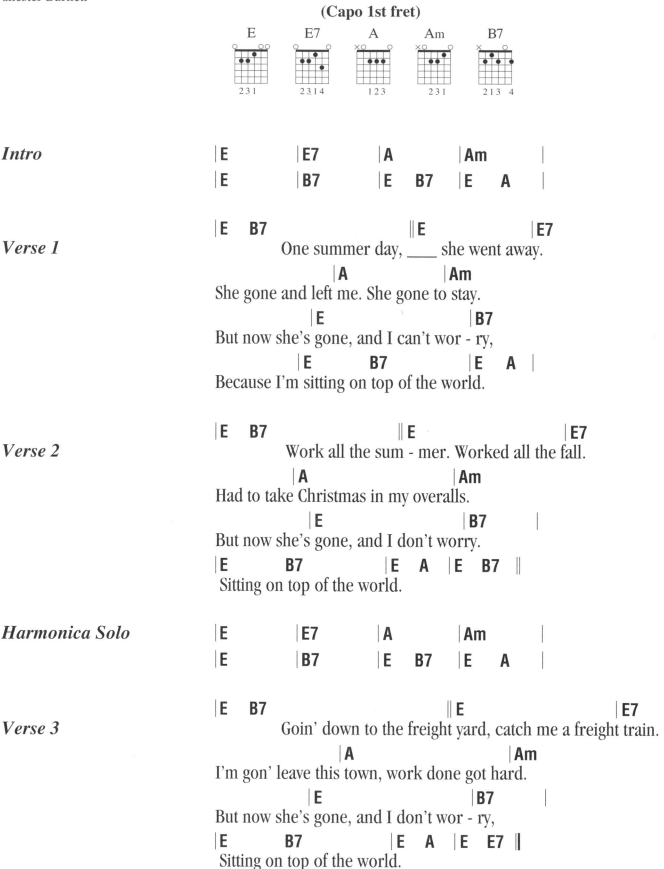

(Capo 1st fret)

Intro

|E |E7 |A |Am |
|E |B7 |E B7 |E A |

Verse 1

|E B7   ‖E |E7
　　　　One summer day, ___ she went away.
　　　　　　|A |Am
She gone and left me. She gone to stay.
　　　　　　|E |B7
But now she's gone, and I can't wor - ry,
　　　　　　|E   B7 |E A |
Because I'm sitting on top of the world.

Verse 2

|E B7   ‖E |E7
　　　　Work all the sum - mer. Worked all the fall.
　　|A |Am
Had to take Christmas in my overalls.
　　　　　　|E |B7 |
But now she's gone, and I don't worry.
|E   B7 |E A |E B7 ‖
Sitting on top of the world.

Harmonica Solo

|E |E7 |A |Am |
|E |B7 |E B7 |E A |

Verse 3

|E B7   ‖E |E7
　　　　Goin' down to the freight yard, catch me a freight train.
　　　　　　|A |Am
I'm gon' leave this town, work done got hard.
　　　　　　|E |B7 |
But now she's gone, and I don't wor - ry,
|E   B7 |E A |E E7 ‖
Sitting on top of the world.

STRUM & SING

Lyrics, chord symbols, and guitar chord diagrams for your favorite songs.

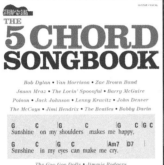

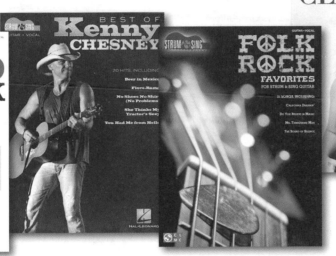

GUITAR

SARA BAREILLES 00102354..................$12.99	**40 POP/ROCK HITS** 02500633..................$9.95	**PRAISE & WORSHIP** 00152381..................$12.99
ZAC BROWN BAND 02501620..................$12.99	**THE 4 CHORD SONGBOOK** 02501533..................$12.99	**ROCK AROUND THE CLOCK** 00103625..................$12.99
COLBIE CAILLAT 02501725..................$14.99	**THE 4-CHORD COUNTRY SONGBOOK** 00114936..................$12.99	**ROCK BALLADS** 02500872..................$9.95
CAMPFIRE FOLK SONGS 02500686..................$10.99	**HITS OF THE '60S** 02501138..................$10.95	**ED SHEERAN** 00152016..................$12.99
CHART HITS OF 2014-2015 00142554..................$12.99	**HITS OF THE '70S** 02500871..................$9.99	**THE 6 CHORD SONGBOOK** 02502277..................$10.99
BEST OF KENNY CHESNEY 00142457..................$14.99	**HYMNS** 02501125..................$8.99	**CAT STEVENS** 00116827..................$10.99
KELLY CLARKSON 00146384..................$14.99	**JACK JOHNSON** 02500858..................$16.99	**TODAY'S HITS** 00119301..................$10.99
JOHN DENVER COLLECTION 02500632..................$9.95	**CAROLE KING** 00115243..................$10.99	**KEITH URBAN** 00118558..................$12.99
EAGLES 00157994..................$12.99	**BEST OF GORDON LIGHTFOOT** 00139393..................$14.99	**NEIL YOUNG – GREATEST HITS** 00138270..................$12.99
EASY ACOUSTIC SONGS 00125478..................$12.99	**DAVE MATTHEWS BAND** 02501078..................$10.95	
50 CHILDREN'S SONGS 02500825..................$7.95	**JOHN MAYER** 02501636..................$10.99	
THE 5 CHORD SONGBOOK 02501718..................$10.99	**INGRID MICHAELSON** 02501634..................$10.99	
FOLK SONGS 02501482..................$9.99	**THE MOST REQUESTED SONGS** 02501748..................$10.99	
FOLK/ROCK FAVORITES 02501669..................$9.99	**JASON MRAZ** 02501452..................$14.99	

UKULELE

COLBIE CAILLAT 02501731..................$10.99
JOHN DENVER 02501694..................$10.99
JACK JOHNSON 02501702..................$15.99
JOHN MAYER 02501706..................$10.99
INGRID MICHAELSON 02501741..................$10.99
THE MOST REQUESTED SONGS 02501453..................$14.99
JASON MRAZ 02501753..................$14.99
SING-ALONG SONGS 02501710..................$14.99

www.halleonard.com
Visit our website to see full song lists.

HAL•LEONARD® CORPORATION
7777 W. BLUEMOUND RD. P.O. BOX 13819 MILWAUKEE, WI 53213

Prices, content, and availability subject to change without notice.

0316

Guitar Chord Songbooks

Each 6" x 9" book includes complete lyrics, chord symbols, and guitar chord diagrams.

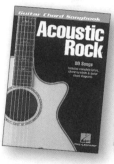  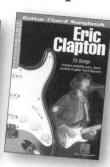 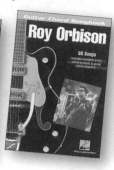 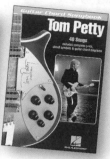 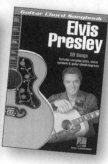 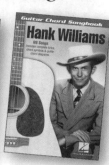

Acoustic Hits
00701787 . . . . $14.99
Acoustic Rock
00699540 . . . . $17.95
Adele
00102761 . . . . $14.99
Alabama
00699914 . . . . $14.95
The Beach Boys
00699566 . . . . $14.95
The Beatles (A-I)
00699558 . . . . $17.99
The Beatles (J-Y)
00699562 . . . . $17.99
Bluegrass
00702585 . . . . $14.99
Blues
00699733 . . . . $12.95
Broadway
00699920 . . . . $14.99
Johnny Cash
00699648 . . . . $17.99
Steven Curtis Chapman
00700702 . . . . $17.99
Children's Songs
00699539 . . . . $16.99
Christmas Carols
00699536 . . . . $12.99
Christmas Songs – 2nd Edition
00119911 . . . . $14.99
Eric Clapton
00699567 . . . . $15.99
Classic Rock
00699598 . . . . $15.99
Coffeehouse Hits
00703318 . . . . $14.99
Country
00699534 . . . . $14.99
Country Favorites
00700609 . . . . $14.99
Country Standards
00700608 . . . . $12.95
Cowboy Songs
00699636 . . . . $12.95
Creedence Clearwater Revival
00701786 . . . . $12.99
Crosby, Stills & Nash
00701609 . . . . $12.99
John Denver
02501697 . . . . $14.99
Neil Diamond
00700606 . . . . $14.99
Disney
00701071 . . . . $14.99

The Best of Bob Dylan
14037617 . . . . $17.99
Eagles
00122917 . . . . $16.99
Early Rock
00699916 . . . . $14.99
Folksongs
00699541 . . . . $12.95
Folk Pop Rock
00699651 . . . . $14.95
40 Easy Strumming Songs
00115972 . . . . $14.99
Four Chord Songs
00701611 . . . . $12.99
Glee
00702501 . . . . $14.99
Gospel Hymns
00700463 . . . . $14.99
Grand Ole Opry®
00699885 . . . . $16.95
Green Day
00103074 . . . . $12.99
Guitar Chord Songbook White Pages
00702609 . . . . $29.99
Hillsong United
00700222 . . . . $12.95
Irish Songs
00701044 . . . . $14.99
Billy Joel
00699632 . . . . $15.99
Elton John
00699732 . . . . $15.99
Latin Songs
00700973 . . . . $14.99
Love Songs
00701043 . . . . $14.99
Bob Marley
00701704 . . . . $12.99
Bruno Mars
00125332 . . . . $12.99
Paul McCartney
00385035 . . . . $16.95
Steve Miller
00701146 . . . . $12.99
Modern Worship
00701801 . . . . $16.99
Motown
00699734 . . . . $16.95

Prices, contents, and availability subject to change without notice.

HAL•LEONARD®
CORPORATION
7777 W. BLUEMOUND RD. P.O. BOX 13819 MILWAUKEE, WI 53213

Visit Hal Leonard online at **www.halleonard.com**

The 1950s
00699922 . . . . $14.99
The 1980s
00700551 . . . . $16.99
Nirvana
00699762 . . . . $16.99
Roy Orbison
00699752 . . . . $12.95
Peter, Paul & Mary
00103013 . . . . $12.99
Tom Petty
00699883 . . . . $15.99
Pop/Rock
00699538 . . . . $14.95
Praise & Worship
00699634 . . . . $14.99
Elvis Presley
00699633 . . . . $14.95
Queen
00702395 . . . . $12.99
Red Hot Chili Peppers
00699710 . . . . $16.95
Rock Ballads
00701034 . . . . $14.99
Rock 'n' Roll
00699535 . . . . $14.95
Bob Seger
00701147 . . . . $12.99
Carly Simon
00121011 . . . . $14.99
Sting
00699921 . . . . $14.99
Taylor Swift
00701799 . . . . $15.99
Three Chord Acoustic Songs
00123860 . . . . $14.99
Three Chord Songs
00699720 . . . . $12.95
Today's Hits
00120983 . . . . $14.99
Top 100 Hymns Guitar Songbook
75718017 . . . . $14.99
Two-Chord Songs
00119236 . . . . $14.99
Ultimate-Guitar
00702617 . . . . $24.99
Wedding Songs
00701005 . . . . $14.99
Hank Williams
00700607 . . . . $14.99
Stevie Wonder
00120862 . . . . $14.99
Neil Young–Decade
00700464 . . . . $14.99

0514

AUTHENTIC CHORDS • ORIGINAL KEYS • COMPLETE SONGS

The *Strum It* series lets players strum the chords and sing along with their favorite hits. Each song has been selected because it can be played with regular open chords, barre chords, or other moveable chord types. Guitarists can simply play the rhythm, or play and sing along through the entire song. All songs are shown in their original keys complete with chords, strum patterns, melody and lyrics. Wherever possible, the chord voicings from the recorded versions are notated.

THE BEACH BOYS' GREATEST HITS
00699357...................................$12.95

THE BEATLES FAVORITES
00699249...................................$14.95

BEST OF CONTEMPORARY CHRISTIAN
00699531...................................$12.95

VERY BEST OF JOHNNY CASH
00699514...................................$14.99

CELTIC GUITAR SONGBOOK
00699265.....................................$9.95

CHRISTMAS SONGS FOR GUITAR
00699247...................................$10.95

CHRISTMAS SONGS WITH 3 CHORDS
00699487.....................................$8.95

VERY BEST OF ERIC CLAPTON
00699560...................................$12.95

JIM CROCE – CLASSIC HITS
00699269...................................$10.95

NEIL DIAMOND
00699593...................................$12.95

DISNEY FAVORITES
00699171...................................$10.95

MELISSA ETHERIDGE GREATEST HITS
00699518...................................$12.99

FAVORITE SONGS WITH 3 CHORDS
00699112.....................................$8.95

FAVORITE SONGS WITH 4 CHORDS
00699270.....................................$8.95

FIRESIDE SING-ALONG
00699273.....................................$8.95

FOLK FAVORITES
00699517.....................................$8.95

THE GUITAR STRUMMERS' ROCK SONGBOOK
00701678...................................$14.99

BEST OF WOODY GUTHRIE
00699496...................................$12.95

JOHN HIATT COLLECTION
00699398...................................$12.95

THE VERY BEST OF BOB MARLEY
00699524...................................$12.95

A MERRY CHRISTMAS SONGBOOK
00699211.....................................$9.95

MORE FAVORITE SONGS WITH 3 CHORDS
00699532.....................................$8.95

THE VERY BEST OF TOM PETTY
00699336...................................$12.95

POP-ROCK GUITAR FAVORITES
00699088.....................................$8.95

ELVIS! GREATEST HITS
00699276...................................$10.95

BEST OF GEORGE STRAIT
00699235...................................$14.99

TAYLOR SWIFT FOR ACOUSTIC GUITAR
00109717...................................$16.99

BEST OF HANK WILLIAMS JR.
00699224...................................$14.99

HAL•LEONARD®
7777 W. BLUEMOUND RD. P.O. BOX 13819
MILWAUKEE, WISCONSIN 53213

Prices, contents & availability
subject to change without notice.

Visit Hal Leonard online at
www.halleonard.com

0316

EASY GUITAR WITH NOTES & TAB

This series features simplified arrangements with notes, tab, chord charts, and strum and pick patterns.

MIXED FOLIOS

00702287	Acoustic	$14.99
00702002	Acoustic Rock Hits for Easy Guitar	$12.95
00702166	All-Time Best Guitar Collection	$19.99
00699665	Beatles Best	$12.95
00702232	Best Acoustic Songs for Easy Guitar	$12.99
00119835	Best Children's Songs	$16.99
00702233	Best Hard Rock Songs	$14.99
00703055	The Big Book of Nursery Rhymes & Children's Songs	$14.99
00322179	The Big Easy Book of Classic Rock Guitar	$24.95
00698978	Big Christmas Collection	$16.95
00702394	Bluegrass Songs for Easy Guitar	$12.99
00703387	Celtic Classics	$14.99
00142539	Chart Hits of 2014-2015	$14.99
00702149	Children's Christian Songbook	$7.95
00702237	Christian Acoustic Favorites	$12.95
00702028	Christmas Classics	$7.95
00101779	Christmas Guitar	$14.99
00702185	Christmas Hits	$9.95
00702141	Classic Rock	$8.95
00702203	CMT's 100 Greatest Country Songs	$27.95
00702283	The Contemporary Christian Collection	$16.99
00702239	Country Classics for Easy Guitar	$19.99
00702282	Country Hits of 2009–2010	$14.99

00702085	Disney Movie Hits	$12.95
00702257	Easy Acoustic Guitar Songs	$14.99
00702280	Easy Guitar Tab White Pages	$29.99
00702212	Essential Christmas	$9.95
00702041	Favorite Hymns for Easy Guitar	$9.95
00140841	4-Chord Hymns for Guitar	$7.99
00702281	4 Chord Rock	$9.99
00126894	Frozen	$14.99
00702286	Glee	$16.99
00699374	Gospel Favorites	$14.95
00122138	The Grammy Awards® Record of the Year 1958-2011	$19.99
00702160	The Great American Country Songbook	$15.99
00702050	Great Classical Themes for Easy Guitar	$6.95
00702116	Greatest Hymns for Guitar	$8.95
00702130	The Groovy Years	$9.95
00702184	Guitar Instrumentals	$9.95
00148030	Halloween Guitar Songs	$14.99
00702273	Irish Songs	$12.99
00702275	Jazz Favorites for Easy Guitar	$14.99
00702274	Jazz Standards for Easy Guitar	$14.99
00702162	Jumbo Easy Guitar Songbook	$19.95
00702258	Legends of Rock	$14.99
00702261	Modern Worship Hits	$14.99
00702189	MTV's 100 Greatest Pop Songs	$24.95
00702272	1950s Rock	$14.99

00702271	1960s Rock	$14.99
00702270	1970s Rock	$14.99
00702269	1980s Rock	$14.99
00702268	1990s Rock	$14.99
00109725	Once	$14.99
00702187	Selections from O Brother Where Art Thou?	$12.95
00702178	100 Songs for Kids	$14.99
00702515	Pirates of the Caribbean	$12.99
00702125	Praise and Worship for Guitar	$9.95
00702155	Rock Hits for Guitar	$9.95
00702285	Southern Rock Hits	$12.99
00702866	Theme Music	$12.99
00121535	30 Easy Celtic Guitar Solos	$14.99
00702220	Today's Country Hits	$9.95
00702198	Today's Hits for Guitar	$9.95
00121900	Today's Women of Pop & Rock	$14.99
00702217	Top Christian Hits	$12.95
00103626	Top Hits of 2012	$14.99
00702294	Top Worship Hits	$14.99
00702206	Very Best of Rock	$9.95
00702255	VH1's 100 Greatest Hard Rock Songs	$27.95
00702175	VH1's 100 Greatest Songs of Rock and Roll	$24.95
00702253	Wicked	$12.99

ARTIST COLLECTIONS

00702267	AC/DC for Easy Guitar	$15.99
00702598	Adele for Easy Guitar	$14.99
00702001	Best of Aerosmith	$16.95
00702040	Best of the Allman Brothers	$14.99
00702865	J.S. Bach for Easy Guitar	$12.99
00702169	Best of The Beach Boys	$12.99
00702292	The Beatles — 1	$19.99
00125796	Best of Chuck Berry	$14.99
00702201	The Essential Black Sabbath	$12.95
02501615	Zac Brown Band — The Foundation	$16.99
02501621	Zac Brown Band — You Get What You Give	$16.99
00702043	Best of Johnny Cash	$16.99
00702291	Very Best of Coldplay	$12.99
00702263	Best of Casting Crowns	$12.99
00702090	Eric Clapton's Best	$10.95
00702086	Eric Clapton — from the Album Unplugged	$10.95
00702202	The Essential Eric Clapton	$12.95
00702250	blink-182 — Greatest Hits	$12.99
00702053	Best of Patsy Cline	$10.95
00702229	The Very Best of Creedence Clearwater Revival	$14.99
00702145	Best of Jim Croce	$14.99
00702278	Crosby, Stills & Nash	$12.99
00702219	David Crowder*Band Collection	$12.95
14042809	Bob Dylan	$14.99
00702276	Fleetwood Mac — Easy Guitar Collection	$14.99
00130952	Foo Fighters	$14.99
00139462	The Very Best of Grateful Dead	$14.99
00702136	Best of Merle Haggard	$12.99
00702227	Jimi Hendrix — Smash Hits	$14.99
00702288	Best of Hillsong United	$12.99

00702236	Best of Antonio Carlos Jobim	$12.95
00702245	Elton John — Greatest Hits 1970–2002	$14.99
00129855	Jack Johnson	$14.99
00702204	Robert Johnson	$10.99
00702234	Selections from Toby Keith — 35 Biggest Hits	$12.95
00702003	Kiss	$9.95
00110578	Best of Kutless	$12.99
00702216	Lynyrd Skynyrd	$15.99
00702182	The Essential Bob Marley	$12.95
00146081	Maroon 5	$14.99
00702346	Bruno Mars — Doo-Wops & Hooligans	$12.99
00121925	Bruno Mars – Unorthodox Jukebox	$12.99
00702248	Paul McCartney — All the Best	$14.99
00702129	Songs of Sarah McLachlan	$12.95
00125484	The Best of MercyMe	$12.99
02501316	Metallica — Death Magnetic	$15.95
00702209	Steve Miller Band — Young Hearts (Greatest Hits)	$12.95
00124167	Jason Mraz	$14.99
00702096	Best of Nirvana	$14.99
00702211	The Offspring — Greatest Hits	$12.95
00138026	One Direction	$14.99
00702030	Best of Roy Orbison	$12.95
00702144	Best of Ozzy Osbourne	$14.99
00702279	Tom Petty	$12.99
00102911	Pink Floyd	$16.99
00702139	Elvis Country Favorites	$9.95
00702293	The Very Best of Prince	$12.99
00699415	Best of Queen for Guitar	$14.99
00109279	Best of R.E.M.	$14.99
00702208	Red Hot Chili Peppers — Greatest Hits	$12.95

00702093	Rolling Stones Collection	$17.95
00702196	Best of Bob Seger	$12.95
00146046	Ed Sheeran	$14.99
00702252	Frank Sinatra — Nothing But the Best	$12.99
00702010	Best of Rod Stewart	$14.95
00702049	Best of George Strait	$12.95
00702259	Taylor Swift for Easy Guitar	$14.99
00702260	Taylor Swift — Fearless	$12.99
00139727	Taylor Swift — 1989	$17.99
00115960	Taylor Swift — Red	$16.99
00702290	Taylor Swift — Speak Now	$15.99
00702262	Chris Tomlin Collection	$14.99
00702226	Chris Tomlin — See the Morning	$12.95
00148643	Train	$14.99
00702427	U2 — 18 Singles	$14.99
00102711	Van Halen	$16.99
00702108	Best of Stevie Ray Vaughan	$10.95
00702123	Best of Hank Williams	$12.99
00702111	Stevie Wonder — Guitar Collection	$9.95
00702228	Neil Young — Greatest Hits	$15.99
00119133	Neil Young — Harvest	$14.99
00702188	Essential ZZ Top	$10.95

Prices, contents and availability subject to change without notice.

HAL•LEONARD® CORPORATION

7777 W. BLUEMOUND RD. P.O. BOX 13819 MILWAUKEE, WI 53213

Visit Hal Leonard online at
www.halleonard.com

0316